Some Other Mother

by AJ Taudevin

Some Other Mother premiered at the Traverse Theatre, Edinburgh on 7 June 2013. This is the text as it went into rehearsal at the Tron Theatre, Glasgow, on 13 May 2007.

ALBA | CHRUTHACHAIL

AT FIFE

Playwrights'
Studio
Scotland

CAST
Star **Shvorne Marks**
Mama **Joy Elias-Rilwan**
Billy/Dog Man **Billy Mack**
Janice/Sarah-Jane **Pauline Knowles**

CREATIVE TEAM
Writer **AJ Taudevin**
Director **Catrin Evans**
Dramaturg **Kieran Hurley**
Designer **Claire Halleran**
Lighting Designer **Laura Hawkins**
Composer & Sound Designer **MJ McCarthy**

PRODUCTION TEAM
Producer **Dani Rae**
Production Manager **Laura Hawkins**
Stage Manager **Mike Heasman**
Technical Stage Manager **Carrie Taylor**

The original production was produced in association with The Scottish Refugee Council and The Tron Theatre, supported by Stellar Quines Theatre company and On at Fife.

The original production featured an original musical score created with contributions from members of LINKES Women's Group and The Women's Creative Company (A Moment's Peace). It was also accompanied by an exhibition of photographs by Robin Taudevin www.robintaudevin.com

Developed with support from Creative Scotland, The Playwrights Studio Scotland, LINKES, A Moment's Peace, Ankur Productions, The Arches and Robin's Fund.

With thanks to Emma McKee, Fiona Sturgeon Shea and the Playwrights Studio Scotland, Niki Logan, Heather McGill and Kirsty Scullin at LINKES, George Aza-Selinger and the National Theatre of Scotland, Hamish Pirie and the Traverse Theatre, LJ Finlay-Walsh and The Arches, Suzi Simpson and the Scottish Refugee Council, Muriel Romanes and Stellar Quines, Helen Belbin, Mara Menzies, Sean Hay, John C Gilmour, Caritas Ndinge, Paksi Vernon, Mary Kapinski, Barbara Rafferty, Callum Cuthbertson, Anita Vettesse, Kirstin Mclean, Kate Bowen, Oliver Emmanuel, Chris Dolan, Noreen Taudevin, Anne Lynch, LINKES Women's Group and The Women's Creative Company.

COMPANY BIOGS

Joy Elias-Rilwan (Mama) appeared in Sally Potter's *The Gold Diggers* whilst still training at Dartington College of Arts. She joined Mike Figis's *The People Show* to do sight specific multi-media experimental physical productions internationally. After three years, the first of her one-woman shows opened at The Meilk Weg Theatre in Amsterdam, The Royal National Theatre afforded her first Shakespeare experience in *A Midsummer Night's Dream* and she created the leading role of a student nurse in the last year of the BBC TV soap *Angels*. Her other theatre roles vary from Lady Bracknell to the lead in *High Life* at the Hampstead Theatre which won her a leading actress award. She was seen in Zenith TV's filmed crime series *991* and in *The Secret Laughter of Women* with Colin Firth. Her voiceover and radio work includes *Talking Books* and *Changes* by Ama Ata Aidoo for BBC Radio 4. She wrote and performed in *Joy, It's Nina*, a film building on the experiences and emotional lives of African women living in the UK separated from their families.

Catrin Evans (director) is a director, writer and activist and works for and with Scotland's leading theatre companies. In the summer of 2013 she is co-writing and co-directing Grid Iron's latest site-specific show *Leaving Planet Earth* with Lewis Hetherington, which will see its World Premiere at the Edinburgh International Festival. Recent directing credits include *Sweet Silver Song of the Lark* by Molly Taylor, *Fragile* by David Greig as part of Theatre Uncut in New York, *Could You Please Look Into The Camera* by Mohammed Al Attar, *Demons* & *The Jeans-Jacques Rousseau Show* by various writers for A Play, A Pie and A Pint, and Associate Director on the National Theatre of Scotland's *Truant* by John Retallack. Catrin is the Artistic Director of political theatre company A Moment's Peace and has co-written and directed all of their shows, including *My Fabulous Tartan Frock*, *The Chronicles of Irania* and *Petrified Paradise*. Catrin also specialises in making performance work within a community context and much of this work has been with asylum seekers and refugees throughout Glasgow.

Claire Halleran (Designer) graduate of Glasgow School of Art and Master of Fine Art, Queen Margaret University. Design credits include *Sex & God*, *After Mary Rose* (Magnetic North),*What Happened Is This*, *Naked Neighbour* (Never Did Nothing), *Paperbelle* (Frozen Charlotte), *The Polar Bears Go Wild*, *Mr Snow*, *The Night Before Christmas*, *Rudolf* (macrobert arts centre), *Forgotten Forest*, *Luvhart*, *First Light*, *My House* (Starcatchers), *Goldilocks* (Platform), *Ignite* (YDance/Smallpetitklein), *Reasons to Dance*, *Allotment* (National Theatre of Scotland), *Hickory and Dickory Dock*, *The Sun*, *The Moon and a Boy Called River* (Wee Stories), *The Pilgrimage*, *Ballerina Ballroom – Cinema of Dreams* (Mark Cousins /Tilda Swinton), *Beneath You* (Birds of Paradise), *Otter Pie* (Fish & Game), *The Art of Swimming* (Playgroup), and various interactive exhibition events for Edinburgh International Science Festival. For images and more information please visit www.clairehalleran.weebly.com.

Shvorne Marks (Star) graduated from Arts Ed in 2011. Theatre includes: *Home* (The Last Refuge), *Trust Fund* (The Bush), *Colour Blind* (Soho Theatre), *Seasoned* (The Tobacco Factory), *'Ave It* (Old Vic Tunnels). Roles while training include Victoria in *Victoria*, Mariana in *Measure for Measure*, Val in *Love and Money*, Joanna in *Present Laughter*, Catherine in *A View From The Bridge*, and Antigone in *Antigone*. Film includes *Cut Loose* and *Fanatical*. Radio includes: *DNA* and *Bridge to the Wounded Heart*.

Laura Hawkins (Lighting Designer & Production Manager) graduated with a degree in Lighting Design from Rose Bruford College. After working as a Technical Manager Laura now works as a freelance Lighting Designer, Technician and Production Manager. Recent credits include Frozen Charlotte, Room 2 Manoeuvre, Plutôt la Vie, Edinburgh International Fashion Festival, Errol White Company, Theatre Cryptic, CackBlabbath Presents, Traverse Theatre and Pitlochry Festival Theatre. Laura also designs and makes jewellery and accessories under the banner of Little Red Star.

Mike Heasman (Stage Manager) has worked in stage management and production management of festivals, theatre and events for the last seven years, and it has taken him from Scotland to New Zealand and back. Recent theatre credits in stage management include *Someone Who'll Watch Over Me*, *Moonlight & Magnolias*, *Twelfth Night*, *Death of a Salesman*, *Proof*, *Jane Eyre*.

Kieran Hurley (Dramaturg) is an award-winning writer, performer, and theatre maker based in Glasgow whose work has been presented internationally and throughout the UK. His monologue *Beats* was developed with the Arches Platform 18 Award and was awarded Best New Play at the Critics' Awards For Theatre in Scotland (CATS). Other works include *Hitch* (Arches, CATS Best New Play nominee), *Chalk Farm* (co-written with AJ Taudevin for Oran Mor, subsequently produced by ThickSkin), and *Rantin* (National Theatre of Scotland/Arches). Kieran is an associate artist with Forest Fringe and is currently on a year-long attachment with the National Theatre of Scotland as recipient of the Pearson Playwrights' Scheme bursary.

Billy Mack (Billy/Dog Man) is an actor living in Stirling, Scotland with his guidwife Calln and their two daughters Mirren and Molly. He became an actor after failing to make a living in the construction industry, then the fishing industry and finally the oil industry. He attended the Royal Scottish Academy of Music and Drama just long enough to graduate in 1995. Since graduating he has worked predominately in Scottish Theatre though his work has taken him to such far flung places as South Africa, Finland, China, Iran and one or two flurries south of the boarder to England. He was the first ever actor to win The Stage Award for Acting Excellence on two occasions, the first for *The Sound of My Voice* in 2009 and the second for *The Overcoat* in 2011.

MJ McCarthy (Composer & Sound Designer) is a Glasgow-based composer, musician & songwriter. Recent theatre work includes *The Day I Swapped My Dad for Two Goldfish* (National Theatre of Scotland), *Un Petit Moliere* (Lung Ha's), *The Winter's Tale* (People's Light, Philadelphia), *Goldilocks* (Platform), *The Authorised Kate Bane* (Grid Iron) & *Educating Ronnie* (Utter/macrobert). Other companies he has worked with include Theatre Uncut, Dundee Rep, Vox Motus and Playgroup. He has toured internationally as a member of the bands Zoey Van Goey and Lord Cut-Glass, and has also composed and recorded several series of radio music for the BBC.

Pauline Knowles (Janice & Sarah-Jane) Theatre includes *The Garden* (Aberdeen Sound Festival), *The Government Inspector, Tam o' Shanter* (Communicado), *Pass the Spoon* (Magnetic North), *Fleeto/Wee Andy* (Best Performer Adelaide Festival, Tumult in the Clouds), *Marilyn* (Edinburgh Royal Lyceum/Citizens), *Matsukaze, Bear on a Chain, A Drop in the Ocean* (Oran Mor), *While You Lie, Gorgeous Avatar, Heritage, Tressel at Pope Lick Creek, Knives in Hens, The Speculator, Marisol, Widows* (Traverse), *Tir na nOg* (Fringe Best New Musical), *Man of La Mancha, Cuttin' a Rug* (Edinburgh Royal Lyceum), *Don Juan, Othello, Cinderella, Wizard of Oz (Citizens), Tutti Frutti* (National Theatre of Scotland), *Liar, Sunset Song, A Scot's Quair* (TAG), *Vassa* (Almeida), *Shining Souls* (Old Vic), *John Brown's Body* (Wildcat/John McGrath). TV Includes: *Case Histories, Personal Affairs, Garrow's Law, Manhunters* (BBC), *Taggart* (STV) and radio includes *The Alterer* (BBC).

Dani Rae (producer) is a freelance producer, dramaturg and consultant. She has worked with and for some of the UK's leading arts agencies and theatre companies including: The Edinburgh Festival Fringe Society, Imaginate, Starcatchers, Gill Robertson, Wee Stories Theatre, Reeling & Writhing, Royal Lyceum, Errol White Company and Plutôt la Vie. Recently Dani worked with Berlin-based contemporary circus producers Circle of Eleven (supported by FST's Producer's Bursary) as booker and PR for their multi award-winning production *LEO*. She also produces for Wolfgang Hoffmann's Aurora Nova Productions managing Nassim Soleimanpour's *White Rabbit Red Rabbit*, Summerhall, Magnetic North Theatre Productions and is currently manager at Bathgate Regal Theatre. **www.danirae.co.uk.**

AJ Taudevin (writer) is associate artist with the Tron Theatre in Glasgow and won the Playwrights Studio New Writers Award in 2010. Her written work includes *Some Other Mother, UNtruth, The YelloWing, Demons, The Jean-Jacques Rousseau Show* and *Chalk Farm. Chalk Farm* was co-written with Kieran Hurley with whom AJ has also collaborated on the creation of *Beats, Hitch* and *Rantin.* As an activist and community arts worker she often works as a Theatre of The Oppressed facilitator and popular educator. She has facilitated and set up women's groups across Glasgow and has been an active member of Glasgow's support network for asylum seekers and refugees since 2007. As actor Julia Taudevin she has worked for theatre companies including The National Theatre, The National Theatre of Scotland, The Traverse, Magnetic North, The Tron, The Arches and A Play, A Pie and a Pint and her screen work includes the feature film *Sunshine on Leith.*

Carrie Taylor (Technical Stage Manager) graduated from The Royal Scottish Academy of Music and Drama in 2006 specialising in stage management and lighting. She has since worked for a range of theatre companies and has been lucky to have had the opportunity to tour a number of shows around Scotland. In 2013 Carrie has worked for Licketyspit Theatre Company, Barrowland Ballet and Shetland Folk Festival, among others. A trained Drama teacher, Carrie has recently written lighting resources for the new National 4 and 5 qualifications to be used by schools in Glasgow City Council.

WRITER'S NOTE

In 2006 my brother, Robin Taudevin, was working as a photojournalist documenting the lives of asylum seekers living in Glasgow. Robin and I grew up in Papua New Guinea and Indonesia, with summers spent at 'home' with my mother's family in the Isle of Lewis. Robin's work with the UN usually kept him working in Indonesia and in East Timor so the opportunity to see him in Scotland was too good to miss so I came up from London, where I was based at the time, to visit him. The people I met through Robin have become some of my dearest friends. I was introduced to a community that was not limited by geography, nationality, race, language, religion or class. I found a kind of solidarity and community I had never experienced before and this played no small role in my moving to Glasgow in 2007.

Shortly after the move, I started working at the LINKES women's group, a weekly drop-in at the high flats on Lincoln Avenue and have worked there ever since. I have facilitated and set up several similar projects across Glasgow. Through these projects I have met hundreds of women, men and children who have been traumatised by the UK's asylum system – regardless of the outcome of their individual claims. I have worked in communities united by a belief in human rights and a more just society, and communities ravaged by the kind of suspicion that is often a byproduct of marginalisation. The structures of support for people in the asylum system are restricted when faced with the brutality of the UK's asylum model. The structures of support for people living in marginalised communities are equally restricted as austerity demolishes the welfare state and lived experience of societal solidarity dies out.

I've known for a long time that I wanted to translate my experience into theatre, but for a long time I struggled to know which story was mine to tell. *Some Other Mother* is entirely my own story in that it is a fiction. But what happens in it is absolutely plausible. Since 2007, I have several times been a support to or advocate for women asylum seekers pushed to the absolute limits of despair as their children have been taken into care by social work because the mothers aren't seen to be coping well enough under the pressures of the asylum system. Dawn raids are still carried out, children are still detained indefinitely or taken into care whilst their parents are detained indefinitely and made vulnerable to deportation without their children, and, of course, deportations continue daily. People are being forced back to countries ravaged by wars fought in my name, plundered by the capitalist exploits of first-world conglomerates and devastated by the legacy of the British Empire.

This play has been inspired by the photographs of my brother who I miss and the stories, hope, joy and determination of my dear friends living in and around the high flats in Knightswood.

SOME OTHER MOTHER

AJ Taudevin

SOME OTHER MOTHER

OBERON BOOKS
LONDON

First published in 2013 by Oberon Books Ltd
521 Caledonian Road, London N7 9RH
Tel: +44 (0) 20 7607 3637 / Fax: +44 (0) 20 7607 3629

A catalogue record for this book is available from the British
Library.

PB ISBN: 978-1-78319-020-1
E ISBN: 978-1-78319-519-0

Cover: photograph by Robin Taudevin

         illustrations by Fogbank.co.uk

inspired by the photographs of my brother
Robin Taudevin www.robintaudevin.com
and the stories of my friends who live or have lived
in the high flats in Knightswood, Glasgow

Characters

Star
a ten-year-old child

Mama
her Nigerian mother

Dog Man
her imaginary friend

Janice
her Glaswegian neighbour

Sarah-Jane
her mother's social worker

Billy
her other Glaswegian neighbour

Some Other Mother is set on a Glasgow high flat estate

and within Star's imaginary world in 2011.

PROLOGUE

STAR stares out of her bedroom window onto the unfamiliar high-rise estate on which she now lives. It is a Glasgow dawn in early summer.

STAR: 'Once upon a time many hundreds of years ago, there was no land, only ocean. Above the world of water flew a great, white bird. A bird as white as the ocean froth, with wings as wide as the sun and eyes as round and deep as the moon. This bird was the wisest and oldest of all birds. It was the albatross. One day the albatross grew heavy. She flew up into the sky and called out to Yemaya, mother of the Orishas "Please ask Oludamare to give me a stretch of land on which I can make a safe home for my babies". Yemaya took the message to Oludamare who smiled on the albatross and granted her wish. And so, for the first time in ten thousand years, the albatross landed...'

BILLY walks out onto his balcony. He stands and watches the sun rise. STAR watches him.

BILLY: We're still staundin, Billy Lithgow. Still staunding. Watched them pull doon the Gorbals wans last year. They say they'll be pullin wan o they Red Road wans doon next. But we'll stay staundin. Jist like the wans in the west. They'll soon be here with their scaffolding and their cladding and their paint and their...

BILLY senses STAR. He turns to see her. Their eyes lock.

STAR: *(Suddenly)* Roar!

STAR hides.

BILLY: God knows I seen them house some strange creatures in these flats but I've never seen them house a baby lion! How on earth did they get her up here? Twelve landings in the sky. Hey wee lion? I know you can hear me. Your windae's wide open. Gonnae tell an auld dug like this wan your tale?

STAR peers over the window.

BILLY: What you saying to it? What sounds like four?

A lion says…
One two three…

STAR: Roar!

BILLY: Woof.

STAR: Roar.

BILLY: Woof!

STAR: Roar!

BILLY: Nice tae meet you too.

There are distant sounds; immigration vans arriving on the estate, the slamming of doors, the pounding of feet on the pavement. They watch.

BILLY: Just you stay locked away behind that windae, hear me? Keep you safe from the lion catchers. See if you'd been here when I was a wean we'd've been down there playing dawn till dusk so we would. Nae bother about nothing. Not a care in the world. See they clatty windaes up the top there? They werenae always closed aff like that. Used to be open. Open to the wind. A blethering communal laundry so it was. All our mammies up in the clouds. Aye, back then it wis brilliant. Back then it was grand.

More distant noise, voices calling, crying, the march of boots, the slamming of car doors. JANICE walks out onto her balcony, on the other side of STAR's window from BILLY.

JANICE: *(Calling to those below)* Nae fuckin way out pals! Nae cunt fuckin escaping.

BILLY: Watch your language, you've a wean for a neighbour now.

JANICE: Welcome to block seven eighty young yin. Where life's wan long shitey symphony of fuck.

BILLY: You're a disgrace, Janice Ucello.

JANICE: Words are the only things we huv, Billy. *(Calling out below)* Isn't that right, pigs? Gonnae come up here and lock away my words?

STAR: Roar.

BILLY: Honest to God, I'll rip your tongue out with my bare haunds if I ever get close to it.

JANICE: I'll jist staund here silent will I? Jist staund here and watch as they tear weans fae breasts o their mothers.

STAR: Roar.

JANICE: Just staund here and watch as they gang about robbin and rapin.

STAR: *(Like a dog.)* Grrarrfk.

JANICE: And pissin and shitein and / fuck fuck cunt fuckin…

STAR: Mama!

JANICE: …in this fuckin cunt hoor cuntish hell that we're stuck in.

BILLY: Janice will ye fuckin shut it…

MAMA enters STAR's bedroom and shuts the window on BILLY and JANICE, shutting out the world outside and closing her and STAR into the bedroom.

MAMA: Shhhh. Irawo, Mama wan bi. Mase oyonu ololufe, Mama wan bi.
(Shhh. Star, Mama is here. Don't worry darling, Mama is here.)

STAR: Mama? Se ole so si fun mi nipa itan Albatross?
(Mama? Can you tell me more of the Albatross story?)

MAMA: *(Wearily)* Albatross? Albatross. Okay. 'Ni igba kan wa…'
('Once upon a time…')

STAR: 'opolupo ogorun odun loju'
('many hundreds of years ago…')

MAMA: '…ibi rara aye…'

('...there was no land...')

STAR: '...kan yoyo okun nlaagbami okun...'
('...only ocean...')

MAMA: '...o ga ju aye igi okun nlaagbami...'
('...and above the earth of waves...')

STAR: '...fifo eye fun fun to tobi.'
(flew a great, white bird.')

ONE

Later the same day, inside STAR's bedroom. It is a bare, drab room. The only furniture is a bed and a packed suitcase on the floor which STAR sits on. There is a huge patch of damp in one of the walls. DOG MAN stands, still and silent inside the damp patch. DOG MAN looks exactly like BILLY, but he is not BILLY. He is DOG MAN.

STAR: '...many hundreds of years ago, there was no land, only ocean. Above the world of water flew a great, white bird. A bird as white as the...'

STAR looks at DOG MAN. They watch each other for a moment, silent.

STAR: 'A bird as white as the ocean froth, with wings as wide as the sun and eyes as round and deep as the moon. This was the wisest of all the birds. It was the...'

There is a loud knock on the front door. STAR jumps up and grabs the suitcase. She listens to the front door being unlocked and opened, then murmuring in the hallway. STAR crouches over her suitcase; an animal ready to flee.

STAR: One... Two... Three...

MAMA enters with SARAH-JANE who is carrying a large file of papers.

MAMA: Irawo? Sarah-Jane niyi. So 'Hello Sarah-Jane'. So 'Hello'.
(Star? This is Sarah-Jane. Say 'Hello Sarah-Jane'. Say 'Hello'.)

STAR: Hello.

SARAH-JANE: Hello. Aren't you just the cutest carbon copy of
your mother?
She looks like you. How old is she?

She consults her notes.

SARAH-JANE: Ten?! Goodness me you're tall. Tall but thin.
We'll need to get you strong for starting high school next
term, won't we? No rubbish. Just lots of good Scottish food
all summer long. My kids would kill for a long holiday
like you're getting, so, believe me, you are one very lucky
young lady.
Your daughter is lucky. She has good luck. Lucky.

MAMA: Thank you.

MAMA goes to exit.

SARAH-JANE: *(Following MAMA)*
Shall we have a wee sit down in the…

MAMA: *(Gesturing for SARAH-JANE to stay)* Please.

SARAH-JANE: It's you I'm here to see Mrs Yewande…

MAMA: *(Going to exit again)* Thank you.

SARAH-JANE: Wait. Wait. Do you understand what I'm saying?

MAMA: Please.

SARAH-JANE: *(Consulting the file)* It didn't… It doesn't say…
Mrs Yewande, I'm terribly sorry. You see, there are
supposed to be two of us for a first visit like this but, well…
um…you've only got me today. And I have no note of you
needing an interpreter. Which you clearly do. Don't you?
Comprendez-vous Anglais?

MAMA: You. Help.

SARAH-JANE: Right.

MAMA: Letter. Please. Help.

SARAH-JANE: I'll need to come back another day.

MAMA: You help. Letter. Come today. Please.

Pause.

SARAH-JANE: Five minutes. I can give you five minutes.

MAMA exits. STAR stares at SARAH-JANE. Pause.

SARAH-JANE: I bet you speak English. Says here you were in London for six months weren't you? See? Not every fish slips through this net. Six months, eh? Must feel like half a lifetime when you're ten. That's a big suitcase you're sitting on. Don't you want to unpack it?

STAR: They move us.

SARAH-JANE: You've only just got here, Stella. You need to start thinking of this as your home.

I suppose ten's a bit too old to play games. It isn't? Do you want to play a little game then?

STAR: Yes.

SARAH-JANE: Do you want to choose something in this room and describe it for me in English?

Beat.

SARAH-JANE: Go on.

STAR points at the damp in the wall where DOG MAN is hiding.

STAR: Black.

SARAH-JANE: *(Slowly)* Damp. We use the word 'damp' for that. Or the word 'mould'. But you're right. It is black in colour. So well done. How about something else now? But maybe this time describe it in a full sentence?

STAR points at DOG MAN inside the wall.

STAR: There is a man in there.

SARAH-JANE: *(Carefully)* You are right. There is a man in the flat next door. Have you met him?

SARAH-JANE opens the blinds and looks out of the window.

SARAH-JANE: Ah. I see. Your window looks right into his balcony. They're doing these flats up soon. Making them nicer. Cleaner. Better. And if the other schemes are anything to go by they'll be getting rid of all the balconies. So when you look out of this window you won't need to worry about seeing anyone. It'll just be you and the sky. Well, and that block in front there. I don't think they're pulling that one down. But at least it'll look nicer than it does now.

MAMA enters with a letter and hands it to SARAH-JANE.

MAMA: Letter. Please.

SARAH-JANE glances over the letter and hands it back to MAMA.

SARAH-JANE: Stella, can you be my little helper? Just for today? Can you tell your mother that she needs to speak to her case worker about this. I can't help her with what's in it. It's not connected to my work with her. Can you tell her that for me?

STAR: Umm. Leta rara di owun.
(The letter is not connected to her.)

SARAH-JANE: Tell her that she needs to ask her case worker for help with this. Okay?

MAMA: Rara di ti owun? Il aye di. To ri leta yi lon ba mi sise!
(Not connected to her? Everything is connected. This letter is the reason for your work with me!)

SARAH-JANE: *(To STAR)* Can you tell me what she's saying please sweetheart?

STAR: She says it's all...um... It's all co...conn... It's all connect...

SARAH-JANE: It's all connected? Can you explain to your mother that I don't work for...

MAMA: Wa da wa pada si ilu wa. Wa wo ilekun wa.
(They will send us back to our country. They'll break in our door.)

STAR: They will send us back. They will break the door.

25

SARAH-JANE: I'm sure that won't happen.

MAMA: Agbodo pada.
(We cannot return.)

STAR: We cannot go back.

SARAH-JANE: I understand that. I do. But I can't help with this.
Your mother's / case worker…

MAMA: So mo ilu wa ti fo?
(Do you know our country is broken?)

STAR: Our country. It is broken.

SARAH-JANE: I know sweetheart, I know. But this letter is from
a completely different government / body from the one I
work for…

MAMA: Egbawa o! Bami fi omo mi obirin pamo fun mi.
(You have to help us. Help me keep my daughter safe.)

STAR: You have to help…keep me safe…for my mamma.

SARAH-JANE: You are safe, Stella.
Stella is safe here.

STAR: But the letter says…

STAR takes the letter from MAMA and tries to read the words.

STAR: De-por-ta-tion…

SARAH-JANE takes the letter from STAR and hands it back to MAMA.

SARAH-JANE: Those words are not for you, okay, sweetheart?
Mrs Yewande. This letter? Home Office. Me? No Home
Office. Understand? Your case worker? Yes? She refer
you to… Your case worker call my off… She… Um. She
telephone me. She say:
Me, Sarah Jane,
help you,
be good
mother
to Stella.

MAMA: *(To SARAH-JANE)*
Irawo.
(Star.)

SARAH-JANE: Sorry?

MAMA: *(To SARAH-JANE)*
Irawo.
(Star)

SARAH-JANE: *(To STAR)*
What's she saying?

STAR: My name.

SARAH-JANE: I thought your name was Stella?

STAR: Mama calls me Star. Irawo. I'm her Star.

MAMA: Irawo. Oruku owun ni Irawo.
(Star. Her name is Star.)

SARAH-JANE: Does your mother always… Is her voice always so forceful?

STAR: She is my Mama.

Beat.

SARAH-JANE: Will you tell her we can talk about this tomorrow when I will bring an interpreter.

STAR: In…ter…?

SARAH-JANE: A translator. Can you tell her that for me, please? My little helper?

STAR: I'owuro to bata.
(Tomorrow she'll bring trainers.)

MAMA: Bata?!

SARAH-JANE: Yes. Bata. So we can talk.

MAMA: Bata?

MAMA and STAR share a moment.

SARAH-JANE: *(To STAR)* What does bata mean?

STAR: Tr…trainers.

SARAH-JANE: What?

STAR: Tomorrow you will bring us trainers.

Beat.

STAR: Like Nike? Adidas?

SARAH-JANE: Thank you, Stella.
Mama? Tomorrow I will bring someone to help with language.
To help us talk.
Your language.
English.
Communicate.
Okay?

MAMA: *(Uncertain)* Thank you.

SARAH-JANE: That's okay. I'm going to go now. I will come back tomorrow.

SARAH-JANE and MAMA exit.

SARAH-JANE: Bye, Stella. Thank you, sweetheart.

MAMA closes the door behind them. STAR sits on the suitcase and listens to the front door closing and locking. DOG MAN emerges from the depth of the wall though, for now, he is still within its confines.

STAR: One. Two. Three.

DOG MAN: Grrrrrr.

STAR: One. Two. Three.

DOG MAN: Grrrrr…

STAR: One. Two. Three.

DOG MAN: Grraarrf.

STAR: *(A new tact)* 'Once upon a time many hundreds of years ago, there was no land, only ocean. Above the world of water flew a great, white bird. A bird as white as the ocean froth, with wings as wide as the sun and eyes as round and deep as the moon. This was the wisest of all the birds. It was the…'

DOG MAN: Albatross.

STAR looks at DOG MAN.

STAR: 'One day the…albatross…grew heavy. She flew up into the sky and called out to Yemaya, mother of the Orishas…'

DOG MAN: '"Please ask God to give me a stretch of land…"'

STAR: 'Olodumare.'

DOG MAN: '"Please ask Olodumare to give me a stretch of land on which I can make a safe home for my weans."'

STAR: 'Babies'.

DOG MAN: 'Weans.'

Beat.

STAR: 'Yemaya took the message to Olodumare…'

DOG MAN: 'Yemaya took the message to…'

STAR: 'Olodumare'

DOG MAN: 'Olodumare who smiled on the albatross and…'

STAR: 'granted'

DOG MAN: 'her'

STAR: 'wish.'

DOG MAN: 'And so'

STAR: 'for the first time in ten thousand years'

DOG MAN: 'the albatross landed and'

STAR: 'made a home for her babies.'

DOG MAN: 'But the weans soon grew hungry.'

DOG MAN / STAR *(Together)* 'Mother Albatross flew out across the ocean to gather food for her weans/babies. She swooped over the waves to find the silver white flash of fish on the ocean surface.'

JANICE: *(Unseen, her voice emerging from the other side of the flat)*
Ya cunting fucking bastard baws.

DOG MAN begins to whimper like a dog.

STAR: Who's that?

JANICE: *(Overlapping, getting louder)* You arseholic cunts wi
your forms and phone calls.

STAR: Is that Yemaya?

JANICE: *(Overlapping)* I jist want tae fuckin see him.

STAR: Mama?

JANICE: *(Overlapping)* Jist want tae know he's awright.

DOG MAN begins to howl like a dog.

STAR: Mama!

JANICE: *(Overlapping)* You bastards care fer nae cunt!

DOG MAN: Ggrrarrghhfk

STAR: Mama? Where's my Mama?

DOG MAN: Your Mama cannot help you. She cannot do a
thing.

JANICE: *(Overlapping)* Nae cunt gies a shite.

DOG MAN: She doesn't speak the language. Closed off from
everything.

STAR: Mama?

DOG MAN: She's a walking skinless eejit bird.
Can't sleep, can't eat, can't understand words.

STAR: Mama!

STAR runs out of the room into the hallway leaving the door open.
DOG MAN retreats.

STAR: *(Hysterical)*
Ronmi Mama. Okunrin! Dog! Okunrin aja!
(Help Mama. Man! Dog! Man dog!)

MAMA enters.

MAMA:Irawo! Oto! Oto!
(Star! Stop! Stop!)

STAR: Okunrin Aja! Aja! Dog Man Dog. Man. Aja. Aja. Man.
Mama
(Man Dog! Dog!)

MAMA: Oto, Irawo. Rara aja. Rara Okunrin. Kantan kantan leyi.
(Stop Star. No dog. No man. This is nonsense!)

JANICE: *(Shouting loud and clear through the walls)*
Hoy! Whit the fuck is goin on in there?

MAMA: *(Calling through to JANICE)*
Ode buruku, kuroni iwaju mi! Fiwa le.
(Bloody fool, fuck off! Leave us alone.)

STAR: Mama…

MAMA: Mama wan bi, Irawo.
(Mama is here, Star.)

JANICE: Dinnae lay a finger on that fuckin wean.

MAMA: Olodumare O, egbawa o.
(Oh God, help us.)

JANICE: You hear me in there? Dinnae lay a fuckin finger on her.

STAR: Mama…

JANICE: I swear I'll fuckin, I'll fuckin…

MAMA: Shhh. Baby. Mama wan bi.
(Mama is here.)

JANICE: Gi me back my wean, ya bastards.

MAMA: Mama wan bi.
(Mama is here.)

JANICE: Gi me back my wean, ya hoors.

MAMA: Mama wan bi. Mama wan bi. Mama wan bi.

Mama wan bi.
Mama wan bi.
Mama wan bi.

A long moment of stillness.

STAR: Mama. I made Yemaya angry.

MAMA: Yemaya?

STAR: The Orisha. The mother of sea and water.

MAMA: Yemaya!

STAR: I can make her forgive me though, can't I?

MAMA: Irawo mi.
  (My Star.)

STAR: She can help us. Can't she? Se Yemaya egbawa?
  (Can Yemaya help us?)

MAMA: Be'ni. Be'ni. Yemaya egbawa.
  (Yes. Yes. Yemaya helps us.)

STAR: We just need to take her a present. Like something nice to eat. And then she helps us.

MAMA: Telemi kalo, ololufe, od'aro.
  (Come with me, darling, let's get you to bed.)

MAMA gently puts STAR to bed.

MAMA: La ala to da, Irawo. Kini won npe ni ede geesi?
  (Dream sweetly, Star. How do I say this in English?)

STAR: You say…dream sweet.

MAMA: Dream sweet.

STAR: Mama? I promise I won't scream again tonight.

MAMA: Irawo mi.

STAR: Star. I'm your star.

MAMA: Dream sweet, mi Star.

MAMA kisses STAR goodnight and leaves the room quietly.

DOG MAN: Grrrrrr.

STAR: Shhh.

DOG MAN: Grrrrrrrrrrr…

STAR: Shut up.

DOG MAN: Grrrarfh.

STAR: I'll feed you to Yemaya.

DOG MAN: Grrmm mmmph.

As the light fades, winds begin to gently buffet and groan. Through the winds YEMAYA, the voice of a thousand women, drifts faintly, barely decipherable, calling:

YEMAYA: Gush the spring, gush the rivers, gush the ocean, gush the waters,
Swirl the waves, swirl the wind, swirl the bodies of my daughters.

TWO

Twelve days later. STAR sits on the suitcase in her bedroom. DOG MAN is still within the wall but he is almost breaking through it. They are more at ease with each other now.

STAR: One… Two… Three…

DOG MAN: What was that?

STAR: One Two Three

DOG MAN: Did you just hear something?

STAR: OneTwoThree

DOG MAN: There's someone at the…

STAR: OneTwoThreeFourFiveSixSevenEight…

DOG MAN: What are you counting?

STAR: Nine Ten Eleven Twelve…

DOG MAN: Ah. Twelve days since we got here.

STAR: No. It's onto the next one anyway.

DOG MAN: The next what?

STAR: The next minute, mumu.
 (idiot.)

DOG MAN: Before what, wee Star?

STAR: Before…

 There is a knock on the front door. STAR immediately grabs her suitcase; poised and ready to flee.

STAR: Is it the letter man?

DOG MAN: How should I know?

STAR: Look.

DOG MAN: I'll look if you promise to start talking to me all the time, not just when you need something from me.

STAR: Mo leri.
 (I promise.)

DOG MAN: Promise.

STAR: I did! Now look.

 DOG MAN becomes Lookout.

STAR: What's Mama doing?

DOG MAN: She's looking through the door flaps…

STAR: She's not getting the clinkyjings?

DOG MAN: She is.

STAR: And opening the clangbangs?

DOG MAN: Uhuh.

STAR: Uhoh.

DOG MAN: One…

STAR: Who is it?

DOG MAN: Two…

STAR: Who's at the door?

DOG MAN: Three…

STAR: Dog Man! Who?

DOG MAN: Grrrrr.

STAR: Who is it?

DOG MAN: Grrrrrrarrrrrfk

STAR: Tell me!

DOG MAN: It's that Sarah-Brain woman.

STAR: She's already been twice this week.

DOG MAN: She's alone this time.

STAR: She hasn't she got Trainers with her?

DOG MAN: Nope.

STAR: Oh no, she'll want me to be her little helper again.

DOG MAN: I'll do the talking.

STAR: You can't.

DOG MAN: Seriously, leave it to me.

STAR: Don't you dare.

DOG MAN: She's coming this way.

STAR: Hide!

MAMA opens the door.

STAR: Quick!

MAMA and SARAH-JANE enter STAR's bedroom. DOG MAN hides. Neither MAMA nor SARAH-JANE ever see DOG MAN.

MAMA: Stella? So 'Hello Sarah-Jane'. So 'Hello'.

STAR: Hello.

SARAH-JANE: Hello. Still not unpacked that suitcase?

Mama, you really need to encourage Stella to make this place a home. We call it nesting here. Like a bird makes a home from twigs and things. A nest.

MAMA: A nest?

SARAH-JANE: Yes, a nest. A bird's nest.

MAMA: You English is too much fast.

SARAH-JANE: I'm sorry. But listen to you! Your English is pretty fast too.

MAMA: Please!

SARAH-JANE: Sorry! Sorry! It's just really good to see how… Your English. It's better. It's good.

MAMA: Thank you.

SARAH-JANE: Thank *you*.

MAMA: You want tea?

SARAH-JANE: Thanks but I'm not here for long.

MAMA: Yes?

SARAH-JANE: I just thought I'd pop in to let you know I've got someone for Stella.

MAMA: Yes tea? No tea?

SARAH-JANE: Oh go on. Just a quick one then.

MAMA: Please you stay here.

SARAH-JANE: I don't have long, Mama.

MAMA: You friend to Stella.

SARAH-JANE: Of course I'm Stella's friend but it's you I need to talk to. You know this.

MAMA: You stay. I bring tea.

SARAH-JANE: Okay. Okay. Remember to leave that door open.

MAMA exits, leaving the door open.

SARAH-JANE: It's not long now till you start high school, is it? You've been so good at keeping up with your numbers. Every time I'm in to see your mum I hear you practising. How far can you count? Do you want to show me? One?

STAR: Two…

DOG MAN: Three…

STAR: Three…

SARAH-JANE: Four? Five?

DOG MAN: Grrrrr.

STAR: *(To DOG MAN)* Shhhh!

SARAH-JANE: Almost. It starts with 'sssss'.

STAR: Six.

SARAH-JANE: That's right. What comes next?

DOG MAN: *(To STAR)* Seven.

SARAH-JANE: *(To STAR)* Seven?

DOG MAN: *(To STAR)* Eight.

SARAH-JANE: *(To STAR)* Eight?

DOG MAN: *(To STAR)* Nine.

SARAH-JANE: *(To STAR)* Nine?

DOG MAN: *(To STAR)* Ten.

SARAH-JANE: Stella? Your mum and I have been doing lots of talking…

DOG MAN: She's hungry, Star.

SARAH-JANE: And we thought you might like somebody of your own to talk to.

DOG MAN: I can hear her tummy rumble.

SARAH-JANE: You can talk about things like, I don't know, what you like to eat.

DOG MAN: She's going to eat you.

SARAH-JANE: Things like, dreams. Good dreams, bad dreams.

DOG MAN: Eat you up and shit you out.

SARAH-JANE: Things like, what wakes you up at night.

DOG MAN: *(Going for SARAH-JANE)* Grrraaffrgh Wrrarffghk!

STAR: *(Lunging at DOG MAN)* Rrrraaaaarrrrr!

SARAH-JANE: Woah there, tiger.

STAR: *(To SARAH-JANE but still holding onto DOG MAN)* Not a tiger!

DOG MAN: Grraarrfghk.

SARAH-JANE: Oops. Not a tiger. Sorry.

DOG MAN: Grrarrfghk.

STAR: Rroaaaarrrarrrrffghk.

MAMA enters, rushing to STAR. DOG MAN retreats into the wall immediately.

MAMA: Irawo! Oto! Oto! Kili ndamu e?
(Star! Stop! Stop! What's wrong with you?)

SARAH-JANE: It's okay, Mama.

MAMA: Kili ndamu e?
(What is wrong with you?)

STAR: There's nothing wrong with me.

SARAH-JANE: She's just playing, that's all.

MAMA: *(To SARAH-JANE)* Please. Every night she is screaming.

SARAH-JANE: It's perfectly normal for a child of her age to play like this.

STAR: Mama?

MAMA: You cannot imagine.

SARAH-JANE: These things take time.

MAMA: She no eat.

SARAH-JANE: Have you made those changes to her diet yet?

MAMA: She no sleep.

SARAH-JANE: Remember what we talked about the other day?

MAMA: She has too much fear inside.

SARAH-JANE: The more rest you can get, the calmer you and Stella will feel.

MAMA: I no can help her.

SARAH-JANE: You cannot help her?

MAMA: She no sleep. I no sleep. I no can help.

Beat.

SARAH-JANE: Are you saying you are refusing to help your child?

MAMA: Please. You help.

SARAH-JANE: I am.

MAMA: You help her.

SARAH-JANE: I have. I am. I've arranged for someone to come visit her. But I think she's doing pretty well all things considered. You need to reconnect. You need to find a way to be calm and relaxed. And that is going to take a lot of hard work on your part. But a mother's work is never done, is it? Do you know this saying? It means, well what it says. A mother's work is never finished. It goes on and on and on and…and we wouldn't have it any other way, would we? We'll come by tomorrow morning, okay?

MAMA: No. Please no morning tomorrow. We have signing. Go Home Office. Week and week and week. Signing name.

SARAH-JANE: Of course you do.

MAMA: Please you come afternoon.

STAR: Mama…?

MAMA: Jo monbo.
(Hold on.)

SARAH-JANE: We'll figure something out. I'd better get on.

STAR: Mama, Dog Man wan bi.
(Mama, Dog Man is near.)

MAMA: Kantan kantan leyi.
(This is nonsense.)

SARAH-JANE: Be gentle with her.

MAMA: Olua o!
(My God!)

SARAH-JANE: Gentle, Mama. Gentle. Gentle voice. Gentle
face. Eyes. Gentle. Gentle.

MAMA: Olua o egbawa o.
(My God help us.)

SARAH-JANE steps back. A beat.

SARAH-JANE: *(Slowly)* I'll show myself out. I'll see you soon.

SARAH-JANE exits.

MAMA: Kili ndamu e?
(What's wrong with you?)

STAR: Dog Man wan bi.
(Dog Man is here.)

MAMA: Rara Dog Man. Woo! Iwo. Emi. Rara aja. Rara
okunrin. Rara Dog Man.
(No Dog Man. Look! You. Me. No Dog. No Man. No Dog Man.)

STAR: He says you don't know how to look after me properly.
He says you don't know how to do it right.

MAMA: Star! He is in you *(indicates her head)* ori. He no…
ododo… He no…

STAR: Real?

MAMA: You say him 'You no real.' You say him 'Which kind
back luck you make me craze so?' You say him 'Go away

from me.' Huh? You say him 'Na. You nothing. I no need you. I am strong. Strong as lion.' Huh?

DOG MAN: *(Emerging)* You tell Mama she can tae get tae fuck.

STAR: *(To DOG MAN)* Ode oshi ashewo.
(You stupid fuck whore.)

MAMA: Stella!

STAR: *(To DOG MAN)* Stupid fuck whore.

MAMA: Malo ede buruku!
(Don't use such bad language!)

STAR: *(Wildly, barking at DOG MAN.)* Grraaarrrfk!

DOG MAN: Grrrarrghghk

STAR: Rrraaaaaaaarrrrrfghk!

JANICE: *(As yet unseen)* Hallo?

MAMA and STAR freeze.

JANICE: Hallo? Are youse awright in here? Ha-llo-o? Can anybody hear me?

JANICE appears in the doorway to STAR's room.

JANICE: Thank fuck, I wisnae sure whit tae expect in here.

MAMA: Out!

JANICE: Your front door was staudin wide open, wumman, do they no tell ye ye cannae dae that here?

MAMA: You dey craze?

JANICE: You're awright, I'm no crazy. I'm jist checkin you're / awright.

MAMA: You go now.

JANICE: I'm goin. I'm gone. I'm jist glad youse are awright.

STAR: You're the one.

MAMA: Irawo!

JANICE: I'm the wan whit?

STAR: You're the one who shouts.

JANICE: You and me both, wee pal.

STAR: Mama wants to kill you.

MAMA: Stella!

JANICE: *(To MAMA)* We've got plenty in common then.

MAMA: She has too much young.

JANICE: Ach, dinnae fash, hen, it's guid tae meet a lassie wi fire in her.

MAMA: You go now.

JANICE: I'm gone.

JANICE hesitates.

JANICE: What's your name by the way?

MAMA: Mama.

JANICE: Right. Does that mean something?

STAR: It means mother.

JANICE: Course it does. I'm jist a stupid auld witch, amn't I?

MAMA: What is shchoopidowuche?

JANICE: Wan day I'll make you a cup o tea and tell ye, how's that, sister?

MAMA: My name is Mama.

JANICE: I know that, sister. Now come on and lock the door behind me, you're no in the jungle noo. Ta ta, wee pal.

JANICE and MAMA exit. DOG MAN slowly comes out of the wall. They listen to the front door closing and locking. MAMA walks back along the hallway into view. She is holding a new letter which she opens and tries to read the words. Only when she has spoken them does their meaning begin to land.

MAMA: 'Application'
'Declaration'

'Asylum Claim'
'Legislation'
'Appeal'
'Exhausted'
'Deportation'
'Sorry. For. Your. Situation'.

*MAMA closes the door to STAR's bedroom. From the other side of the
door, MAMA starts to cry. DOG MAN begins to come out of the wall.*

DOG MAN: 'Mother Albatross flew out across the ocean to
gather food for her weans.'

STAR: 'She swooped over the waves to find…'

DOG MAN: '…the silver white flash of fish on the ocean
surface.'

STAR: 'She gathered up the fish in her beak and…'

DOG MAN: '…in amongst the silver white flash of fish were the
silver white flashes of lighters and bottle tops and broken
glass. The mother albatross, couldn't tell the difference
between these new kinds of flashes and the flashes of fish.'

STAR: No. Dog Man, no, 'She gathers up the fish in her beak
and wings her way back to her babies. / The starving baby
albatrosses sing for joy when they see their mother. They
open up their beaks and flap their feathers and gulp down
the juicy…'

DOG MAN: 'The starving baby albatrosses sing for joy when
they see their mother. With their paper thin bellies
shivering with hunger they gulp down the silver white
shards of glass and lighters and bottle tops. Their throats
split as they swallow.'

STAR: One…

DOG MAN: 'Their stomachs rip and tear and the marble shards
of dinners gone by crumble out of the babies' broken
bodies filling their nest with the crunch of shredded guts
and broken glass.'

STAR: One two…

DOG MAN: Have you looked in your food little star? Is your mama feeding you lighters and pen lids and razor blades?

STAR: One two three…

DOG MAN: Is she feeding you glass? Is she ripping you apart piece by piece without knowing?

STAR: One.

DOG MAN: What is that pain in your tummy little Star?

STAR: Two.

DOG MAN: Is that the first rip?

STAR: Three.

DOG MAN: The first cut of the blades?

STAR: ROAR.

STAR attacks DOG MAN.

STAR: I'll feed you to Yemaya. She'll have you for dinner.

DOG MAN: She doesn't exist, ya doolally wee scunner.

STAR: She does. She's the mother of the great Orishas,
Who keep the world turning and look after us.
There's Oyu. He rules wind and guards the gates of death.
There's Oshun. She rules fresh water and brings the rain to earth.
But Yemaya, she's the greatest. She rules the ocean and seas.
She's mother to every single thing. And she's always hungry.

The light fades and winds begin to whip and howl. Through the winds YEMAYA, the voice of a thousand women, swirls, louder but still barely distinguishable, calling:

YEMAYA: Rip the wind, rip the rain, turn my children's world to pain.
Flow the water over sand, flood the valleys, flood the land.

THREE

Fourteen weeks later. STAR sits on the suitcase in her bedroom. DOG MAN is no longer in the wall. They are entirely familiar with each other inside STAR's bedroom now. There is the sound of construction work from outside.

STAR: One...Two...Three...Four...Five...Six...Seven...Eight... Nine...Ten...Eleven...

DOG MAN: Twelve thirteen fourteen weeks.

STAR: I'm not counting the weeks, bawbag.

DOG MAN: Oh. Are you counting the bangs from the diggers out there?

STAR: Bang. Clang. Scrape.

DOG MAN: I hate that scraping sound. Gies me the derubas.

STAR: What did you say?

DOG MAN: Derubas. It's Yoruba for heebeejeebees.

STAR: Heebee...

DOG MAN: Heebeejeebees. Mama taught me.

Beat.

STAR: Onetwothreefourfivesixseveneightnine...

DOG MAN: Don't you ever get bored?

STAR: Don't you ever get eaten?

DOG MAN: Apparently not.

STAR: Stay with me long enough and you will.

DOG MAN: You're lying.

STAR: *You're* lying.

DOG MAN: I can't lie. I'm an adult.

STAR: You don't look like an adult.

DOG MAN: I do. I look like Stupid old Witch.

STAR: No you don't.

DOG MAN: And I look like Sarah-Brain.

STAR: You look nothing like either of them.

DOG MAN: They all look the same.

STAR: Witch is much uglier than Brain.

DOG MAN: Shame you're not Brain's clever little helper anymore. It doesn't matter how many pictures you draw and cards you make for her, she still says you're not allowed to help.

STAR: It's not because I'm not allowed to. She says it's because I'm not an apricot.

DOG MAN: You mean she says it's not appropriate.

STAR: I mean she says you should shut up because you don't know what you're talking about and you should get tae fuck. Don't you dare laugh at me. I'm strong! I'm strong as a lion! Stop laughing like that you…you…you…you nothing dog.

DOG MAN: Wmf.

STAR: You're pure mental by the way.

There is a knock on the front door. They look at each other, uncertain for a moment. Then assume the Lookout position. This is a routine they are very familiar with now.

DOG MAN: Mama's looking through the letter flaps…

STAR: Is it them?

DOG MAN: It's not them.
She's getting the clinkyjings. And opening the clang-bangs. Who could it be? One. Two. Three. It's… It's…

STAR: Who? Who's at the door?

DOG MAN: Grhmph. Witch.

STAR: They're total bezzies now.

DOG MAN: What's that about?

STAR: Fuck knows.

There is a soft knock on STAR's bedroom door and MAMA enters, DOG MAN hangs back but does not disappear. JANICE stands in the hallway. MAMA is much changed. She is exhausted after weeks of worry and uncertainty.

MAMA: Stella, Jannie here.

JANICE: Awright skinny malinky longlegs?

DOG MAN: *(Quietly.)* Grrrrr…

MAMA: Say 'Hello Jannie'.

DOG MAN: Grrrrrrrrr…

MAMA: Say 'Hello'.

JANICE: Ach, it's no bother. I wouldnae say boo to a goose when I was your age.

MAMA: What is Bootoagoose?

JANICE: They are words you do not need to worry aboot, sister.

STAR: That's not her name.

JANICE: I know that, you wally.
Come on, you. Let's have a look at the words you *dae* need worry aboot.

MAMA: *(Leaving the bedroom)* I tell you, Jannie, they want to destroy me.

JANICE: I know they do, hen. I know.

MAMA and SARAH-JANE exit and close the door.

STAR: 'One day the albatross grew heavy. She flew up into the sky and called out to Yemaya, mother of all Orishas…'

DOG MAN: You do know you can't remember the end of that story.

STAR: *(Honestly)* You do know you smell of wee.

DOG MAN: That's hardly my fault.

STAR: Lookia fudface, you're not real, so go away.

DOG MAN: They're coming to get you. The letters have spoken.

They'll fly you both back to your land that is broken.

STAR: Why are you speaking like that?

DOG MAN: Like what?

STAR: Like her.

DOG MAN: Like who?

STAR: *(Meaning YEMAYA)* Like *her.*

DOG MAN: But I'm you.

There is a loud knock on the front door. They freeze. Then assume the Lookout position.

STAR: Is it them? Have they come for us?

DOG MAN: Mama's looking through the letter flaps...

STAR: They can't send us back, Dog Man. They have to let us stay here.

DOG MAN: Shhh. I can't hear what Mama and Witch are saying.

STAR: It can't be them. They take you in the morning. Or when you are signing.

DOG MAN: They're getting the clinkyjings.

STAR: We need to find Yemaya.

DOG MAN: Opening the clangbangs...

STAR: We need to find the way.

DOG MAN: One...

STAR: We need to ask her to help us.

DOG MAN: Two...

STAR: Before it's too late.

DOG MAN: Three...

STAR: Who is it? Is it them?

DOG MAN: No. It's Brain.

STAR: Sarah-Brain? Something's wrong.

DOG MAN: Witch is leaving. Brain is coming in.
She's asking lots of questions.

STAR: Oh, please no, not again.
What does she want? What is she asking?

DOG MAN: Same as always. I'll be her.
I'll be Sarah-Brain.

STAR: I'll be Mama.

DOG MAN: 'How are you feeling? How are you doing?
How are you reeling? How are you pooing?
How are you coping? How are you reaping?
How are you hoping? How are you sleeping?'

STAR: 'Spoonfuls.'

DOG MAN: 'Spoonfuls of what?'

STAR: 'Of sleep.'

DOG MAN: 'I'm lost.'

STAR: 'Night and night and night, awake with fear.'

DOG MAN: 'You need to sleep, you need to persevere!'

STAR: 'My life is like…'

DOG MAN: 'What's it like?'

STAR: 'Like…'

DOG MAN: 'Like…?'

STAR: 'Like…death.'

DOG MAN: Death?

STAR: That's what Mama just said.

Beat.

DOG MAN: She just said the word death.
Was that the word she used?
That's not a word to use like that.
The Brain'll get confused!

STAR: One...

DOG MAN: It's pouring.

STAR: Say one.

DOG MAN: It's sleeting.

STAR: Dog Man, say one.

DOG MAN: And Mama...

STAR: One.

DOG MAN: is greeting.

STAR: Say one!

DOG MAN: One.

STAR: Two.

DOG MAN: Three.

STAR/DOG MAN: *(Together)* Roar!

> *A soft knock. SARAH-JANE enters. MAMA stays in the hallway, she is falling apart.*

SARAH-JANE: Stella? Are you okay in here?

DOG MAN: Will I go for her? Will I take a wee bite?

STAR: *(To DOG MAN)* No!

SARAH-JANE: What's wrong? What's happened?

DOG MAN: A wee chunk o her bum. Just tae gi her a fright.

STAR: *(To DOG MAN)* Don't do it.

SARAH-JANE: Don't do what?

DOG MAN: *(Going for SARAH-JANE, who does not see him)*
Grrrrrrrraaarr. Wrrraaarrfghk. Wrrrraaarrrfghk.

STAR: *(Wildly, trying to distract SARAH-JANE from seeing DOG MAN)* I made this, I made it for you. Look. I drew it all on my own. No help. Not one bit of help. Look!

SARAH-JANE: Oh! Another card. What is it this time? A pussy cat?

DOG MAN: Grrrr…

STAR: No!

SARAH-JANE: A lion?

DOG MAN: Wrrrarrfk.

STAR: No no no!

SARAH-JANE: Calm down Stella.

DOG MAN: Grraaarrrfk. Grrrarrrfk!

STAR: Shut up.

SARAH-JANE: Stella, do I need to count to three?

DOG MAN: Grrrr.

STAR: He's a dog.

SARAH-JANE: Of course it's a dog. You always draw a dog.

DOG MAN: It's going to eat you up.

STAR: *(To DOG MAN)* No it isn't, shut up.

SARAH-JANE: Stella?

STAR: *(To SARAH-JANE)* Not you…

DOG MAN: It's going to eat you up and shit you out.

SARAH-JANE: I'm going to count to three.

STAR: *(To DOG MAN)* Shut it.

SARAH-JANE: One…

DOG MAN: Lion.

STAR: *(To DOG MAN)* Shut up.

SARAH-JANE: Two…

STAR: *(To DOG MAN)* I said shut up.

SARAH-JANE: Two and a half, Stella…

DOG MAN: Lion!

STAR: *(To DOG MAN)* Shut the fuck up or I'll kick your fucking cunt in.

SARAH-JANE: Do *not* speak to me like that, young lady.

STAR and DOG MAN freeze.

STAR: *(To SARAH-JANE)* Was that bad?

SARAH-JANE: You do not speak to people like that. Now apologise immediately. Apologise!

DOG MAN: *(To STAR)* I'm sorry

STAR: *(To DOG MAN)* I'm sorry.

SARAH-JANE: Stella, come on. You are better than this.

STAR: Please don't take me away.

Beat.

SARAH-JANE: Can you come in here please, Mama?

MAMA enters the bedroom, nervous, on the edge. DOG MAN stays out of her way.

SARAH-JANE: Do you mind if I tell Stella a bit more about what it is you're agreeing to? Is that okay? Okay.

We haven't been talking about taking you away, Stella. We've been talking about you taking a wee holiday. We all think you're doing brilliantly and that it would be great to give your mum a wee rest. A wee break. A holiday. Just for a couple of weeks.

STAR: A holiday?

SARAH-JANE: Yes, sweetheart. A wee holiday in a place that is so good it's got a sand pit. A sand pit! And if everything goes to plan you'll be going there in the next couple of days. And you can make sandcastles for the rest of the summer, well what little is left of it. Doesn't that sound good?

STAR: What's sandcastles?

SARAH-JANE: A sandcastle is a castle made of sand.

STAR: Will my mama have one?

SARAH-JANE: Your mother's going on a special holiday of her own. Isn't that right, Mama?

MAMA: Please.

SARAH-JANE: You're doing really well, Mama.

MAMA: We need to be together.

SARAH-JANE: This isn't a separation. It's a chance to get some rest.

MAMA: In London last week they take woman in detention centre but not baby. People from your work they take her baby.

SARAH-JANE: I don't think that's true.

MAMA: It is true. A woman from Sudan!

SARAH-JANE: That sort of thing doesn't happen.

MAMA: Maybe they send this woman back Sudan without her baby.

SARAH-JANE: That won't happen.

MAMA: You say you are not from Home Office.

SARAH-JANE: I'm not, you know I'm not.

MAMA: So how can you know they will not send her back without her baby?

SARAH-JANE: Mama, we're getting sidetracked here. I'm not sending you back anywhere without Stella. I'm just suggesting you take a short break before the school term starts. It's not forever.

MAMA: Thanks be to God!

SARAH-JANE: It's the only thing I can do for you that will ensure you get some rest, Mama.

MAMA: Maybe yes this sleep drug holiday make me have day and night no thinking. Maybe yes this fun time holiday make my baby laughing. But there is too much fear inside. If we are not together the fear become too much strong. It break us.

SARAH-JANE: Respite. You need respite. You'll find it so much easier to cope.

MAMA: But when still the letters come?

SARAH-JANE: They won't come as long as you're in the hosp… As long as you're on holiday.

MAMA: And come the day the holiday finish? Next day I look to the door? Again letter. Again. Again. Again. Refuse. Refuse. Refuse.

SARAH-JANE: You know I can't change that.

MAMA: We cannot go back. For us this is like death. We wait for the letter from them that say we can stay. You say you cannot make this good news letter come.

SARAH-JANE: I can't.

MAMA: You say it is good for me I go holiday. Sleep holiday from my baby. Sleep holiday from bad news letter. Okay. But the day this holiday stop? We waiting again for good news letter. Again we waiting. Again night and night and night we fear. Again night and night and night we no sleep. Again you come back here. Again you say I am not this coping.

SARAH-JANE: Mama. You're not coping. You've said so yourself. You know that's why I'm here.

MAMA: You are here because this good news letter not come. You are here because we live inside fear. You want I take sleep holiday from this fear? Okay. Maybe then you see that this not coping is not from me bad mother. Maybe then you see that this not coping is from fear. We live inside fear. This holiday? It cannot stop this fear.

SARAH-JANE: You're doing the eye thing you do, Mama.

MAMA: You say my child is suffer. Yes. My child is suffer. But not from me bad mother. My child is suffer because the fear is too much strong it get in her head, in her heart, in her body. You tell me how I can get out this fear from her when this same fear is too much strong in me? Huh?

SARAH-JANE: Stop doing the eye thing.

MAMA: You tell me how you can help me be good mother when you cannot make better this fear? Huh?

SARAH-JANE: Your eyes, Mama.

MAMA: These are my eyes. I cannot stop them being my eyes.

SARAH-JANE: They are frightening to the child.

MAMA: This is my child. My baby. My life. I am not this fear for her.

SARAH-JANE: Your voice is extremely aggressive.

MAMA: This is my voice. How can I make you hear it?

SARAH-JANE: You are frightening Stella.

MAMA: Stella, baby, comia to mummy.

DOG MAN: Grrrrrr.

MAMA: Stella? Baby?

STAR does not go to MAMA. Beat.

MAMA: Her skin. It is not like your skin. No oil and it go dry. It go white. Like bird feather. You take her this fun time holiday, how you stop this feather skin fly away? Huh? How you stop this feather skin fly away in the wind?

SARAH-JANE: It's only for a couple of weeks. I urge you to agree, Mama. It will make things so much easier.

MAMA: Irawo, comia to Mama.

STAR: Does Mama get a sandy bit?

SARAH-JANE: What's that, sweetheart?

STAR: The thing you make the castles in. Does Mama get one?

SARAH-JANE: Pit. A sand pit. It's a pit. With sand in it. It's a holiday thing. A play thing. A fun thing.

DOG MAN: She's thinks we're doolally.

SARAH-JANE: Doesn't that sound good?

STAR: We're not stupid.

SARAH-JANE: I know you're not stupid.

DOG MAN: The lion catcher's a liar.

STAR: Why do you speak to us like we are?

SARAH-JANE: I don't.

DOG MAN: Lying Liar.

SARAH-JANE: I…

DOG MAN: Aye?

SARAH-JANE: I…

DOG MAN: Aye?

SARAH-JANE: I… I need to go. I have more visits to do.

DOG MAN: One…

SARAH-JANE: You need to agree, Mama. This is your best option.

DOG MAN: Two…

SARAH-JANE: It's only a few weeks till she starts high school.

DOG MAN: Three…

SARAH-JANE: You'll both come back relaxed. Rested. Ready to face what ever is ahead.

DOG MAN: One…

SARAH-JANE: I'll lend Stella a plastic bucket of her own to make sandcastles.

DOG MAN: Two…

SARAH-JANE: Are we agreed?

DOG MAN: Three…

MAMA: Okay.

STAR: Four.

MAMA: What more can I say? Okay.

SARAH-JANE: Thank you. They start work on this block
tomorrow. You'll come back and they'll have put a nice
thick layer of cladding on the outside. New paint on the
walls. No more of that horrible damp. It'll be like, I don't
know, like paradise. Compared to what it is now, anyway.
You know, things are so much better than they used to be
for people in your situation, Mama. Only four, five years
ago, things used to be very, very difficult. And the more we
communicate, the more we work together, people like you
and me, the easier things become. For all of us. I should be
able to wrap things up in time to move on this tomorrow.
You will find it easier to cope after this rest. I promise.

Bye bye Stella. Sleep well tonight. Come on, Mama, see
me to the door. That's it.

SARAH-JANE and MAMA exit, closing the door behind them.

*DOG MAN becomes Lookout to watch them go. STAR stays sat on the
suitcase; still and silent.*

DOG MAN: She's saying goodbye to Mama. She's ready to go.
She's closing the door… Three two one… Kabloomo!
Goodbye Shite-pie. Just you get tae fuck.

There is the faint sound of MAMA crying.

DOG MAN: It's raining.
It's sleeting.
And glaikit Mama's greeting.

STAR: Right. That's it. There's no more time to waste.
I'll write a letter to Yemaya and take it to the Orisha place.

DOG MAN: You'll never get there. You don't know the way.
And it's not long till bed time, till the end of the day.

STAR: Perfect timing, she'll be up. Watching over the world.
We'll give her a letter to take to God and offer her in return
A gift of things she likes to eat...
Things like rare, unusual meat.

*STAR opens the suitcase and starts rummaging, throwing her things
around the room.*

DOG MAN: What are you doing? You can't unpack. Didn't you
hear her? You're not here to stay.
And what if they come for you in the morning? And you
don't get your holiday?

STAR: We'll write 'Dear Olodamare, how's it going? Can you
help us?
The Brain's a bit confused about what's really in those
letters.
Like the albatross, we need a safe place we can be.
But somewhere we're together, my Mama and my me.'

*There is a knock on the front door. DOG MAN freezes, expecting STAR
to assume the Lookout position, but STAR is too busy looking for pen
and paper. DOG MAN completes the routine on his own.*

DOG MAN: *(Hushed voice)* Mama's looking through the flaps...
Is it them?
It's not them.
She's getting the clinkyjings. And opening the clang-bangs.
Who could it be? One. Two. Three. It's... It's...

JANICE: *(Calling)* It's Janice.

DOG MAN: Huh. Fannychops.

*STAR is totally unaware of DOG MAN as she sits on the suitcase
writing the letter to Olodumare. Unimpressed, DOG MAN returns
inside the wall. JANICE enters.*

JANICE: You awright wee pal?

STAR hides the letter.

JANICE: It's jist me. Your mammy's through there getting the kettle on. Nothin like a good bang o the gums to make you feel better. What about yoursel? Gonnae gi your ain gums a wee bang for us?

STAR looks to DOG MAN. JANICE follows her gaze.

JANICE: Do you know something? I have a photie somewhere of me when I was younger. I'm sittin at the windae, right? My wee Davey on my knee. And the wall behind me in the photie is just beginning to go black wi the mould. I mean, imagine that, eh? Imagine that wall there, what, ten year back. Imagine it being mare paint than damp. Can you imagine that?

STAR: I hear people call you things. What do they call you?

JANICE: Folk call me all sorts o hings. But my name is Janice.

STAR: What do I call you?

JANICE: You can call me aunty. If you want?

Beat.

JANICE: See, Star, it's hard being on your ain wi a wean. You'll no doubt learn that yoursel wan day. But jist think, what if we were family? What if we all ganged the gether? Stood up against they folk in charge? Looked oot for wan another? Heart to heart. Like family, aye? Like sisters. Like brothers. You've got nae uncles here have ye? Nae aunties?

STAR: Just me and my Mama.

JANICE: Well, as your Scottish auntie, I am givin you full permission tae call me whatever the fuck you like.

Now, I don't know about you but I've got a right drouth. Gonnae come through and say night-night tae your mammy?

Come on then, wee pal. Hey. It's all going to be okay.

They exit. DOG MAN stays in the wall, uncertain. STAR runs back in, still holding the letter for YEMAYA.

STAR: Dog Man? You still there?

DOG MAN: Aye.

STAR: We'll find the Orishas and Yemaya tonight.
Will you come? Please. I need you.

DOG MAN: Do you? Oh.
Alright.

STAR: Promise?

DOG MAN: Promise.

STAR: Good. Now don't go anywhere.
We'll go after I've kissed Mama goodnight
So she doesn't get worried and scared.

STAR exits.

*As the scene fades, the winds begin to rip and roar and YEMAYA, the
voice of a thousand women, howls:*

YEMAYA: Gush and swirl and rip and flood
My children fish in pools of blood.

ROAR

*Much later that night. STAR and DOG MAN are in the world of the
Orishas, looking for YEMAYA. It is a strange and constantly shifting world
which looks more and more like STAR's bedroom as the scene progresses.*

STAR: Hello? Is anybody there?

DOG MAN: Nope. Naebody. Let's go home.

STAR: Not yet. We've got all night.

DOG MAN: This place gi's me the derubas.

STAR: *(Shouting)* Is there no one else in this whole world that
can hear me?

DOG MAN: *(Howling)* Halloooo!

*The wind begins to rip through the Orishas' world – like a storm at
sea. YEMAYA, the voice of a thousand women, is never seen.*

YEMAYA: Gush the spring, gush the rivers, gush the ocean, gush the waters.
Swirl the waves, swirl the wind, swirl the bodies of my daughters.

DOG MAN: Home time.

STAR: We can't go home. We've come too far.
You'll be fine. You do the talking.
You're better at that than me.

DOG MAN: Oh no. No chance. There was a sign back there
A sign! Didn't you see?

STAR: What sign?

DOG MAN: It says No Dogs Allowed.
Perishable By Death!

STAR: Ah.

DOG MAN: So you had better do the chat.

STAR: Okay. Let me catch my breath.
Hello Oh wind-erful Yemaya
Please forgive my friend's woofish face
but it's taken us a full ten thousand years
to get to this Orisha place.
I've got a message / for Olodumare...

YEMAYA: 'Dear Olodumare, how's it going? Can you help us?
The Brain's a bit confused about what's really in those letters.
Like the albatross, we need a safe place we can be.
But somewhere we're together, my Mama and my me.'

STAR: She already knows.

YEMAYA: Rip the wind, rip the rain, turn my children's world to pain.

DOG MAN: *(Whimpering like a dog)* Arroooo...

YEMAYA: Flow the water over sand, flood the valleys, flood the land.

STAR: Mama? Where's Mama? Mama? Mama! Mama!
Where's Mama? Where's Mama?

DOG MAN: She's gone. We left her. Left her far behind.

STAR: You be Mama, please, Dog Man. Please.

DOG MAN: No you be Mama, I can't be.

STAR: If I am Mama, then who'll be me?

DOG MAN: You don't matter.

YEMAYA: Gush and swirl and rip and flood
My children fish in pools of blood.

STAR: Quick!

*DOG MAN becomes MAMA, cradling STAR. DOG MAN speaks in a
different language – not Yoruba. The wind howls.*

DOG MAN: Shhh. Mon petit irawo. Mama est nibi. Maman wa
la. Mama wa here.
*(Shhh. My darling Star. Shhhh. Mama is here. Mama is here.
Mama is here.)*

STAR: Mama?

DOG MAN: 'Ni igba kan wa, many huners d'années
auparavant, there wasnae nae de terre, only…only. One…
duex…tres…roar. Okun. Okun. L'eau. Bird. Okun. Ucello.
Seulement. Une. One. Une. Two. Three. One. Two. Three.
Above du monde, roar. Du monde. The l'eau. The ucello
grand. Les ifo eye fun fun blanc. Un two tres ucello blanc
de l'eau waves. Les okun saggio Une. Ucello. Two. Okun.
Tres…'

STAR: Mama?

DOG MAN: '…The sun et les yeux…les yeux…les yeux'

STAR: Mamaroooooo.

DOG MAN: les yeux

STAR: *(Howling like a dog)* Arrooooooo.

DOG MAN: Les Eyes!

STAR: *(Howling like a dog)* Arraarraaarrooooo.

DOG MAN: Eyes!

STAR: What?

DOG MAN: Use Mama's eyes.

YEMAYA: 'Like the albatross, we need a safe place we can be.
But somewhere we're together, my Mama and my me.'

DOG MAN: Mama's voice. Use Mama's voice.

STAR: Please. Help us. Please.

YEMAYA: Who's your me?

STAR: My Me?

DOG MAN: She's me.

YEMAYA: Who?

STAR: Me.

YEMAYA: You?

DOG MAN: We.

YEMAYA: Who?

STAR: We?

DOG MAN: She.

YEMAYA: If she is 'me', then who is he?

STAR: Mama.

DOG MAN: I'm not Mama! *She's* Mama!

YEMAYA: Bye bye birdie. Off you fly.

STAR: What? Where are you taking her?

YEMAYA: That's classical information. Say good bye.

DOG MAN: If it's Mama you're after, that's her right there.
Mama's nose. Mama's skin. Mama's eyes. Mama's hair.

STAR: Oh no, no no no no no.
I'm not Mama. I'm… I'm…

I'm…

A plastic bucket appears.

DOG MAN: Say 'Hello Stella', say 'hello'!

STAR: *(Into the plastic bucket)* Hello Stella.

DOG MAN and STAR begin to tap and bang on the side of a plastic bucket.

STAR: Hello Stella!
Hello Star!
Are you happy so far far far
far far far far away?
Are you happy on your fun time holiday?

DOG MAN's tapping builds until he is bashing and banging the plastic bucket around the room.

DOG MAN: Are you happy, Stella oh Stella oh Star?
Happy on your sand pit holiday?
You don't need to come back for morning time
They will only just take you away
Back to the land that is broken and fucked
The land the letters tell you is safe.
Stay where you are, Star, you're much better off
Sarah-Brain has always been right.
You don't need your Mama to look after you
You're far too clever and bright.

DOG MAN's banging of the bucket becomes the sound of people banging on the front door. MAMA enters STAR's bedroom, in real time. STAR is still in the world of the Orishas and MAMA tries to bring her back into reality.

MAMA: Stella?

DOG MAN: Mama!

STAR: *(To DOG MAN)* Stay! Dog Man! Stay!

DOG MAN races wildly around the room, howling, wild, bewildered, lost.

MAMA: Stella! Stop! Oto! Stop!

STAR: *(Turning on MAMA)* You crazy fuck nut bitch.

MAMA: Stella, baby.

STAR: You lying monster mother.

MAMA: Stella. My baby. My Star.

STAR: You thieving bastard voodoo witch!

MAMA: Mama wa nib, Star. Mama is here.

STAR: You can't be a mother.

MAMA: They have come, baby. They are here.

STAR: You can't be anything.

> *The banging on the front door is louder. JANICE's voice can be heard over the banging, shouting from inside her flat.*

JANICE: *(Her voice, through the walls)* Ya mother-fuckin-cuntin-fucks lay aff my sister's door.

STAR: Olodumare doesn't exist.

JANICE: Have you nae mothers? Nae family?

STAR: And Yemaya's a stupid whore!

JANICE: Have you nae weans?

STAR: I'm going to eat you. On the count of three.

MAMA: Star. My baby.

JANICE: Have you nae hearts?

MAMA: God. You destroy us.

STAR: One…

JANICE: Shame on you!

MAMA: Please help, God, please.

STAR: Two…

JANICE: Shame!

MAMA: We are on our knees!

JANICE: Shame!

MAMA: Our skin is flapping.

STAR: Two and a half...

MAMA: Flapping in the wind.

JANICE: Shame!

STAR: THREE

> *There is a crash as the front door is smashed in. All of STAR's imaginary torments, including DOG MAN, vanish completely. A brief moment of calm.*

STAR: Mama? They are here, aren't they?

MAMA cradles STAR.

MAMA: Mama wa nibi, Irawo.
Mama is here.
Mama wa nibi.
Mama wa nibi.
Mama wa nibi.
Mama wa nibi.

EPILOGUE

Later the same day. As in the prologue: STAR's window, BILLY's balcony, JANICE's balcony. STAR is not at her window. Her room is strewn with the rubble of last night. BILLY walks out onto his balcony. The sounds of construction is constant.

BILLY: Get a whiff o that, Billy Lithgow. Woooft. That is the stench of a dying era. Nae hearses yet, though, Billy. No fae the likes of us. Mare's the pity. Knock em doon. That's whit I say. Knock us all doon and bury us all.

JANICE walks out onto her balcony.

BILLY: Was that you this morning Janice? Banging and shouting and screaming? Given up the good samaritan act, have you? Knew it wouldnae last. A craikit bell'll never mend. And your bell's craikit right through in't it? In't it? Hey? What you sayin tae it? Not like you tae gi that tongue o yours a rest.

JANICE: I cannae find it, Billy.

BILLY: There is a God!

JANICE: The photie.

BILLY: He's answered wur prayers and ripped oot her tongue!

JANICE: Billy! The photie! I cannae find it.

BILLY: Hallelujah!

JANICE: The photie, Billy, the photie. It's the only wan I've got o my wee Davey.

BILLY: Ach, change the record, ya auld witch, the Wee Davey wan's been playin ten year.

JANICE: We're sitting at the windae. The wall behind us jist beginning tae go black wi the mould. And see, the photie is that dark, it could be anyone sitting there. Any mother. Any wean. But I cannae find it. I want to see if that mother is me or if it aye could be some other. Some other wean upon the lap of some other mother.

BILLY: You were born spoutin shite, Janice Ucello.

JANICE: They've took them, Billy. They're gone. The mama and the wean. They've sent them back from where they came. We'll never see them again.

The sounds of construction builds.

BILLY: Well cryin and hallooin like that's never goin tae change a thing.

JANICE: *(Shouting)* Words are the only things I huv, Billy.

BILLY: Cannae hear you ower that racket, Janice. Cannae hear a word.

JANICE: *(Calling out to those below)* Aye, go on ya herd o shiteflaps. Jist you seal us intae silence. Jist you seal us intae toxic walls, jist you make us look aw nice and white. So nae cunt'll know the truth aboot whit's goin on inside us.

BILLY: Dinnae bother wi that paint, pal. Knock us doon! Bury the lot o us.

JANICE: Jist you lock us in and wall us aff so you'll think we're aw awright. While they bastards whit own us dae whit ever they like tae folk whit live beside us. Nail ower wur doors. Paint ower the cracks. There's nae body we can tell. Whit cunt'll listen tae me? Inside this castle of sand. Inside these walls you're paintin sae white against the grey sky black.

Blackout.